Swahili Guide

The following is meant to give a basic understanding of the structure and vocabulary of Swahili, so that you can get around on the streets of Tanzania. It's in no way comprehensive and there are even intentional errors (for simplicity's sake), but it will prepare you to hold everyday conversations and provide a foundation to build upon. Again, it's not perfect and other supplements are necessary, but I wish I'd had something like this before heading over. I give some pronunciation guides, but things are spelled phonetically and almost always pronounced as you would think. The Swahili alphabet uses the English alphabet (except for "q" and "z").

For a brief history, Swahili (Kiswahili) is spoken by approximately 80 million people across Eastern and Central Africa. It's an official language in Tanzania and Kenya, but is also spoken in Uganda, Rwanda, Burundi, and parts of Somalia, Zambia, Mozambique, and the Democratic Republic of the Congo. It's the second most commonly understood language in Africa, behind Arabic, and is used as a lingua franca to connect all of the various tribal languages in that region.

So let's get started.

Greetings to any age group:

Habari yako? (ha-bah-ri ya-koh) – How are you?

Habari za asubuhi/mchana/jioni? – How's your morning/afternoon/night?

Responses:

Nzuri! (en-zoo-ri) – Good! (this response is used 96% of the time, even if you aren't "good"…)

Salama! (sa-lah-mah) – Peaceful!

Poa! (poh-ah) – Cool!

Respectful greetings to older/important people:

Shikamoo (shee-kah-moh) – literally means "I touch your feet," but don't worry, it's not weird to say

Response:

Marahaba (ma-rah-ha-bah) – "I am delighted"

Greeting to tourists:

Jambo! (jahm-boh) – Hello!

Response:

Jambo! (if you don't know Swahili) *or* Sijambo! (if you know a little bit of Swahili)

Common slang greetings to your own age group:

Mambo vipi? (mahm-boh vee-pee) – How are problems? (used like "what's up?")

Uko poa? – You cool? (as in, "are you doing alright?")

Responses:

Poa – Cool (most widely used response)

Safi – Clean

Safi sana (sah-fee sah-nah) – Very clean (to show the use of the adjective "sana," which emphasizes your point and is placed behind, like in Spanish)

Mzuka – Ghost (not used often, but used)

Shwari (slang response without a real translation)

From here on out, I'm mostly not adding pronunciations. Don't worry, people will help you figure it out. The important thing is to recognize the words and structure.

Farewells for any age group:

Kwaheri – Good-bye

Kesho – Tomorrow

Baadaye – Later

Useful Words:

Asante (sana) – Thank you (very much)

Karibu – for "you're welcome" and "welcome to Tanzania"

Verb Introduction:

To quickly break down a common verb (which I'll further explain as I go), let's look at how you would say "I am going."

Ninaenda

To break that into the three main pieces:

Ni-na-enda

Ni – I

Na – Am

Enda – Going

So as you can see, "I am going" is squeezed into one word with three components – person, tense, and action. Fortunately, this is how every single sentence/verb is structured in Swahili, and there are only a handful of exceptions.

So let's first look at the first section of the verb, or the personal pronoun section.

Personal Pronouns

Mimi – I/Me

Wewe – You

Yeye – He/She/Her/Him

Sisi – We/Us

Ninyi – You all (y'all)

Wao – They/Them

Personal Pronouns in Verbs

Each of the above pronouns has a marker that is used in verb construction. For instance, in our "ninaenda" example, the "ni" prefix represented "I." The following correspond to each person:

Ni – I (Mimi)

U – You (Wewe)

A – He/She (Yeye)

Tu – We (Sisi)

M – You all (Ninyi)

Wa – They (Wao)

Again, in our example, we used the "ni" prefix for:

Ninaenda

If we had wanted to say "you all are going," it would be:

Mnaenda

(pronounced "mmm-na-enda – get used to this kind of consonant-consonant pronunciation)

For "he/she is going," it would be:

Anaenda

Here's a test - write in the book.

How do you say "we are going"…"

_____

And so on. See? Easy. Please note that in Tanzania, they DO NOT say "Mimi ninaenda." That's like saying "I, I am going" and is quite redundant.

For the "I" person, they often even leave out the "ni." Don't get confused, but when saying "I am going," people often say "naenda," leaving off the "ni" prefix. Saying "ninaenda" isn't wrong, people think that the "ni" is already implied. Keep in mind that this only is the case with the "I" tense – the other five all require their respective u/a/tu/m/wa prefix.

Tense Markers in Verbs

Now let's move on to the second part of the verb, or the "na" in our "ninaenda" example. This middle component signals the tense of the action, and "na" signals present tense.

The following are the four major tense indicators. Though there are others, you'll rarely hear them in everyday conversation.

Na (nah) – present

Li (lee) – past

Ta (tah) – future

Me (meh) – present perfect

To apply each of these to our example:

Ninaenda – I am going/I go

Nilienda – I was going/I went

Nitaenda – I will be going/I will go

Nimeenda – I have been going/I have gone

Action markers in Verbs

The third section of the verb, which is our running example is "enda," signals the action involving the person/tense prefix/infix.

To begin, all verbs start in their infinitive form, with a ku-prefix. In the case of "ninaenda," the root infinitive is:

Kuenda

Every verb can be recognized in its infinitive form with the ku- prefix, and that prefix is simply removed when the first two components of a working verb are inserted. So the formula for turning "kurnda" into "ninaenda" was:

What verb? Kuenda.

Great, take off the ku-prefix. Now we have –enda.

Who is doing the action? I am.

Great, so we'll use a ni- prefix.

When are you doing that action? Right now. The present.

Great, so we'll use a –na- infix.

Now let's piece it all together:

Ni-na-enda.

Done.

BEST OF ALL, it's literally that simple for every verb. It's a formula – find your person, find your tense, remove the ku- prefix from your verb infinitive and splice it all together. The verb ending doesn't change in fifty million conjugations for seventy-eight different tenses with four-hundred and three exceptions (like other languages, English included), it follows a simple formula and stays the same no matter if I am doing the action now or he will be doing the action tomorrow or if they have been doing the action all along.

I'll provide a list of commonly used verbs later, I just think it's handy to introduce the structure before discussing common phrases, so that you can break down any verbs you may see into the three parts and better understand them.

Common Phrases

Throughout these phrases, I insist on trying to literally translate the phrases into English. You'll understand when to use them, but I don't like when phrasebooks just give you the gist in English or the English slang equivalent – yes, that tells you when it's appropriate to use those phrases, but it kills any attempt at actually learning the language's structure.

Unatoka wapi? – You are from where?

Ninatoka Merikani. – I am from America.

Unatoka nchi gani? – You are from which country?

Ninatoka Merikani. – I am from America.

(Remember, verbs come after nouns, so in the above example, "nchi" is "country" and "gani" is "which")

Unatoka mji gani? - You are from which city?

Ninatoka Lynchburg. – I am from Lynchburg.

Unaitwa nani? – You are called who?

Ninaitwa John. – I am called John.

Jina lako ni nani? – Your name is who?

Jina langu ni John. – My name is John.

To briefly pause and point something out, in the above examples, you can see that "jina" is the Swahili word for "name." It's followed by "lako" in order to signal "your" or "langu" to signal "my."

"Lako" and "langu" do not universally mean "your" and "my" in showing possession. They change prefixes depending on the world. We'll get to it later, but for now, recognize "-ako" as "your" and "-angu" as "my." In this case, they both have an "l" in the front, corresponding to the rules for "jina." Here's a list:

My - -angu

Your - -ako

His/Her - -ake

Our - -etu

Your (pl) - -enu

Their - -ao

Again, I'm not dwelling on it yet, and it's not really something you need to know to get around on a day-to-day basis, but below are some examples

Mtoto wangu – my child

Jina langu – my name

Mtoto wake – his child

Jina lake – his name

Chakula changu – my food

Chakula chenu – Your (pl) food

As you can see, it's confusing. There are different "noun classes" and adjectives are altered to fit their noun class in the same way many languages change their verb endings to fit the tense or person. It's not as complex, and there aren't as many noun classes, but it's similar. Noun classes are organized in similar groups – like one for words related to people, one for words related to animals and nature, etc.

That's the trickiest part of Swahili, and something I don't have a full grasp on yet. I wanted to bring it up so that you have an idea as to why it seems like adjectives change for different words, but I don't want to dwell on it. If you said "jina wangu" for "my name" instead of the proper "jina langu," people would know exactly what you meant and wouldn't fault you.

So don't worry about being that technically perfect just yet. Let's get back to some common phrases.

Unajua Kiingereza? – Do you know English?

Ndiyo. – Yes

Unajua Kiswahili? – Do you know Swahili?

Hapana. – No

Kidogo. – A little.

Tafadhali – Please

Pole – Sorry

Samahani – Excuse me

Msaada! – Help!

Unasemaje…kwa Kiswahili? – How do you say…in Swahili?

Nataka kujifuna Kiswahili. – I want to learn Swahili.

Choo/Bafu iko wapi? – Choo/Bathroom is where?

Hoteli iko wapi? – Hotel is where?

Glacier iko wapi? – Glacier is where?

Benki iko wapi? – Bank is where?

Hii ni bei gani? – This is which price?

Chilingi ngapi? – How many shillings?

Ghali (sana) – Expensive (very)

Rahisi (sana) – Cheap (very)

Naomba bia. – I would like a beer.

Naomba chakula. – I would like food.

Chakula ni nzuri. – The food is good.

As another quick note, there are no articles in Swahili – the nouns stand alone. "Bia" can refer to the abstract concept of beer, "a beer," "the beer," etc. There is no a/an/the word in Swahili, which takes some getting used to. Demonstratives and pointing also help.

Numbers

Numbers in Swahili are extremely important for everyday life, providing the necessary link in being able to haggle around with prices and pay like the locals. Keep in mind that 1 USD is the same as ~1600 Tanzanian Shillings, so it's important to understand how to say amounts in the thousands. "Chilingi" is generally the appropriate word for monetary amounts, so it's thrown in front of all following numeric amounts to demonstrate a price.

Sifuri - 0

Moja – 1

Mbili – 2

Tatu – 3

Nne – 4

Tano – 5

Sita – 6

Saba – 7

Nane – 8

Tisa – 9

Kumi – 10

Mia – 100

Elfu – 1,000

Milioni – 1,000,000

Those are the basics, and the rest is easy. In order to say 2,000, you'd piece together "elfu" (1,000) and "mbili" (2), for "elfu mbili." It follows the same pattern as noun-adjective. To say 500, it'd be "mia tano." To say 2,500, it's "elfu mbili, mia tano." Easy enough.

To add on the missing pieces:

Ishirini – 20

Thelathini – 30

Arobaini – 40

Hamsini – 50

Sitini – 60

Sabini – 70

Themanini – 80

Tisini – 90

In order to tie everything together, we need the word "na," which means "and." This isn't the same as the –na- infix for constructing verbs, and is also used to mean "with."

In order to say eleven, it's:

Kumi na moja – 11

As you can see, it's literally translated to "ten and one." The same pattern remains for the rest of the numbers…

Themanini na nane – 88

Arobaini na nne – 44

And so on. To make it a bit more complex,

Elfu mbili mia tano arobaini na nne – 2,544

The "na"/"and" only pops up for the space between the tens and ones digit. You don't need it for the rest of the spaces.

So for use in conversation:

A: Hii ni chilingi ngapi? – This is how many shillings?

B: Hii ni chilingi elfu mbili. – This is 2,000 shillings.

A: Nataka kulipa elfu moja mia tano. – I want to pay 1,500.

B: Poa. Asante. – Cool. Thank you.

To round things out, here are some related vocabulary for use with numbers:

Nusu – ½

Robo – ¼

Asilimia – Percentage

Nambari – Number

Numbari ya simu – Number of phone

Ngapi? – How many?

Mwaka/Miaka – Year/Years

Una miaka ngapi? – You have how many years?

Nina miaka ishirini na moja. – I have 21 years.

Days of the Week

To quickly run through them, here are the days of the week.
The "first day" of the week is Saturday.

Siku – Day

Wiki - Week

Jumamosi – Saturday

Jumapili – Sunday

Jumatatu – Monday

Jumanne – Tuesday

Jumatano – Wednesday

Alhamisi – Thursday

Ijumaa – Friday

Months of the Year

And here are the months of the year. As with days of the week, you can find bits of the counting numbers within the structure.

Mwezi - Month

Mwezi wa kwanza – January

Mwezi wa pili – February

Mwezi wa tatu – March

Mwezi wa nne – April

Mwezi wa tano – May

Mwezi wa sita – June

Mwezi wa saba – July

Mwezi wa nane – August

Mwezi wa tisa – September

Mwezi wa kumi – October

Mwezi wa kumi na moja – November

Mwezi wa kumi na mbili – December

Those are the technical names, but you can usually Swahili-ize the English names and get away with it.
December=Desemba, February=Februari, March=Machi, etc.

Noun Classes

As I mentioned before, there are several different noun classes that comprise different segments of vocabulary. Each of them structures any accompanying adjectives in a unique way. I'm honestly not sure exactly how many different classes there are (it seems to change depending on the source), but I'm going to highlight six. They are as follows:

Class 1 - M/Wa

Class 2 - Ki/Vi

Class 3 - M/Mi

Class 4 - Ji/Ma

Class 5 - N/N

Class 6 - U/U

These are named by the singular/plural form of the associated nouns. For instance, "mtu" means person and "watu" means people. This is a Class 1 noun and uses that suffix –tu with either a singular m- prefix or a plural wa- prefix.

Note that this is different than mwaka/miaka (year/years), which is a Class 3 noun. It's unfortunately not as easy as what letter the word begins with, though it becomes easy to pick up on patterns.

I'm not going to heavily focus on the different adjective agreements with each noun class, as that's easily forgiven while learning Swahili. Those language skills are a long way down the line, so I'm choosing to focus on the basics so that after a little bit of time, you're pretty competent.

Noun Class 1 – M/Wa

This noun class encompasses nouns associated with people (with m/wa prefixes), other nouns associated with people (without m/wa prefixes), and some animals.

Mtu/Watu – Person/People

Mtoto/Watoto – Child/Children

Mgeni/Wageni – Foreigner/Foreigners

Mkulima/Wakulima – Farmer/Farmers

Msichana/Wasichana – Girl/Girls

Mvulana/Wavulana – Boy/Boys

Mzungu/Wazungu – Tourist/Tourists

Mwalimu/Walimu – Teacher/Teachers

Mwanafunzi/Wanafunzi – Student/Students

Mwaafrika/Waafrika – African/Africans

Rafiki – Friend(s)

Mnyama/Wanyama – Animal/Animals

Mbwa – Dog(s)

Paka – Cat(s)

Simba – Lion(s) [yes…like The Lion King]

Kuku – Chicken(s)

Mbu – Mosquito(es)

Noun Class 2 – Ki/Vi

This class includes random nouns that follow the ki/vi pattern or the ch/vy pattern of singular/plural. It also encompasses many body parts and the names of different languages.

Kitu/Vitu – Thing/Things

Kiti/Viti – Seat/Seats

Kitabu/Vitabu – Book/Books

Kiatu/Viatu – Shoe/Shoes

Kisu/Visu – Knife/Knives

Kikombe/Vikombe – Cup/Cups

Kitanda/Vitanda – Bed/Beds

Choo/Vyoo – Toilet/Toilets

Chakula/Vyakula – Food/Foods

Chumba/Vyumba – Room/Rooms

Kichwa/Vichwa – Head/Heads

Kifua/Vifua – Chest/Chests

Kidole/Vidole – Finger/Fingers

Kiarabu – Arabic

Kiingereza – English

Kifaransa – French

Kichina – Chinese

Noun Class 3 – M/Mi

This class includes trees and plants, some more body parts, nouns that follow the m/mi pattern, and a few exceptional cases that follow the same general idea.

Mti/Miti – Tree/Trees

Mmea/Mimea – Plant/Plants

Mdomo/Midomo – Mouth/Mouths

Mkono/Mikono – Hand or Arm/Hands or Arms

Mguu/Miguu – Foot or Leg/Feet or Legs

Moyo – Heart

Mwili/Miili – Body/Bodies

Mfano/Mifano – Example/Examples

Mji/Miji – City/Cities

Mtihani/Mitihani – Exam/Exams

Mlima/Milima – Mountain/Mountains

Mungu/Miungu – God/Gods

Mpira/Mipira – Ball/Balls

Mchezo/Michezo – Game/Games

Mwezi/Miwezi – Month/Months

Mwaka/Miaka – Year/Years

Mwisho/Miwisho – End/Ends

Noun Class 4 – Ji/Ma

This noun class encompasses manufactured products and abstract/concrete concepts, even more parts of the body, many fruits, natural objects, and some various ma- prefixed nouns.

Gari/Magari – Car/Cars

Sanduku/Masanduku – Box/Boxes

Duka/Maduka – Shop/Shops

Shamba/Mashamba – Farm/Farms

Soko/Masoko – Market/Markets

Jina/Majina – Name/Names

Kosa/Makosa – Mistake/Mistakes

Neno/Maneno – Word/Words

Jambo/Mambo – Problem/Problems

Wazo/Mawazo – Thought/Thoughts

Swali/Maswali – Question/Questions

Jicho/Macho – Eye/Eyes

Tumbo/Matumbo – Stomach/Stomachs

Embe/Maembe – Mango/Mangoes

Chungwa/Machungwa – Orange/Oranges

Yai/Mayai – Egg/Eggs

Maji – Water

Noun Class 5 – N/N

This noun class also includes manufactured products and abstract/concrete concepts, as well as foods, fruits and vegetables. In this tense, the singular and plural versions of the nouns are the same.

Chupa – Bottle(s)

Barua – Letter(s)

Dawa – Drug(s)/Medicine(s)

Kalamu – Pen(s)

Karatasi – Paper(s)

Suruali – Trouser(s)

Soksi – Socks

Nguo – Cloth(s)

Dola – Dollar(s)

Taa – Light(s)

Kompyuta – Computer(s)

Nyumba – House(s)

Baridi – Cold

Barafu - Ice

Barabara – Road

Njia – Way

Nchi – Country

Ajali – Accident

Bahati – Luck

Hatari – Danger

Furaha - Joy

Dakika – Minute(s)

Biashara – Business(es)

Ndoto – Dream(s)

Nguvu – Strength(s)

Sifa – Praise(s)

Hasara – Loss(es)

Chai – Tea

Kahawa - Coffee

Chumvi – Salt

Pilipili – Pepper

Mboga – Vegetable(s)

Ndizi – Banana(s)

Nyama – Meat(s)

Siagi – Butter

Sukari – Sugar

Noun Class 6 – U/U

This class contains concrete nouns, uncountable nouns, nouns that are formed with a "u" from adjectives, and the names of many countries.

Uso – Face

Uma – Fork

Ndevu – Beard

Nywele – Hair

Ufunguo/Funguo – Key/Keys

Ukuta/Kuta – Wall/Walls

Upande/Pande – Side/Sides

Wakati/Nyakati – Time/Times

Wimbo/Nyimbo – Song/Songs

Umeme – Electricity

Umri – Age

Usingizi – Sleep

Ujamaa – Community

Utoto – Childhood

Upendo – Love

Uingereza – England

Ufaransa - France

Verbs

So now that you have a basis for vocabulary, let's revisit verbs. As a reminder, the formula for conjugating verbs for tense and person is the same for all verbs, with only a few exceptions.

Firstly, the exceptions. These are "monosyllabic" verbs, and are still very easy to conjugate. Basically, you leave on the ku- prefix when adding in the other bits.

Kula – To eat

Kunywa – To drink

Kuja – To come

Kufa – To die

For example, "nitakula" means "I will eat." Not "nitala." Again, for these shorter verbs, the ku- remains.

The verb for "to be," kuwa, is also an exception. The present tense for ALL persons is simply "ni."

Ni – I am

Ni – You are

Ni – He/She is

Ni – We are

Ni – You (pl) are

Ni – They are

Easy enough. And for the past/present, it acts monosyllabic.

For example, "I will be" is "nitakuwa." Just like "I will eat" is "nitakula." Same idea for past tense.

The other notable exception is the verb for "to have." It's quite simple, though, as it's taught in Swahili as "to be with," and tacks a "na" onto the end of the normal conjugations for "kuwa." As a reminder, "na" is the Swahili word for "and" or "with." So "I will have" can be thought of as "I will be with," and is written "nitakuwa<u>na</u>."

But other than those, there really aren't any exceptions. All of the remaining verbs follow along with the simple three part formula. Below are listed some of the most common verbs:

Kutaka – To want

Kuhitaji – To need

Kununua – To buy

Kuuza – To sell

Kufanya (kazi) – To do (work)

Kujua – To know

Kusema – To say

Kuongea – To converse

Kuambia – To tell

Kucheka – To laugh

Kutambea – To walk

Kukimbia – To run

Kufika – To arrive

Kuacha – To leave

Kuenda – To go

Kuendesha – To drive

Kufunga – To close

Kufungua – To open

Kuchukua – To take

Kuchagua – To choose

Kukaa – To stay

Kukata – To cut

Kupika – To cook

Kuleta – To bring

Kungoja – To wait

Kupenda – To like/love

Kusafisha – To clean

Kusimama – To stop

Kuomba – To ask nicely for

Kutafuta – To search for

Kuweka – To put

Kuweza – To be able

Kulala – To sleep

Kuamka – To wake up

Kuanza – To begin

Kupiga – To hit

Kusamahe – To forgive

Kukumbuka – To remember

Kugeuza – To turn

Kufikiri – To think

Kufarahi – To be happy

Kusafiri – To travel

Kuketi – To sit

Kushinda – To win

Kushindua – To lose

Kujaribu – To try

Kujibu – To answer

Kukamata – To hold

Kutazama – To look at

Kuona – To see

Kuangalia – To look (like)

Kuanguka – To fall

Made in the USA
Middletown, DE
22 October 2023

41216260R00019